CUTE
EMERGENCY

CUTE
EMERGENCY

TONY HEALLY

THREE RIVERS PRESS

NEW YORK

All rights reserved. Published in the United States by Three Rivers Press, an imprint of the Crown Publishing Group, a division of Penguin Random House LLC, New York.

www.crownpublishing.com

Three Rivers Press and the Tugboat design are registered trademarks of Penguin Random House LLC.

Originally published in hardcover in different form in Great Britain by Bantam Press, an imprint of Transworld Publishers, Penguin Random House Ltd., London, in 2014.

Library of Congress Cataloging-in-Publication Data
Heally, Tony.
  Cute emergency / Tony Heally. — First edition.
      pages cm
  1. Animals—Humor. 2. Animals—Pictorial works. I. Title.
  PN6231.A5H43 2015
  818'.602—dc23
                                    2015007068

ISBN 978-1-101-90462-6
eBook ISBN 978-1-101-90463-3

Printed in China

Cover photographs by Shutterstock
Photograph credits appear on pages 167–169.

10 9 8 7 6 5 4 3 2 1

First U.S. Edition

CONTENTS

INTRODUCTION

Having a rough day? Well, you've come to the right place. This book is full of adorable animals who can lend a helping paw in any Cute Emergency. There are sleepy kittens, dogs in sweaters, bunnies, ducklings, you name it—no matter what kind of stressful situation you're in, you're bound to find a furry friend in these pages. (Or a prickly one. We didn't forget you, hedgehogs.)

HE FELL ASLEEP DOING
YOGA *AGAIN*.

0-2:
Low

A low-level Cute Emergency may be caused by: Your coffee shop being out of your favorite muffin, your sweater sleeve getting all wet when you wash your hands, or the frustration of trying to fold a fitted sheet. Stay calm. Cute animals are here to help.

"IT SMELLS OKAY. I MEAN, IT'S NO FIRE HYDRANT, BUT . . ."

"CHEEEESE!
NO, BUT SERIOUSLY,
IS THERE CHEESE?"

♪ "I THINK WE'RE ALONE MEOW." ♪

"MY NEST OR YOURS?"

"WHO *SAYS* WE'VE SETTLED IN THE LOOKS DEPARTMENT?"

"I CAN'T GO OUT THERE. SADIE IS WEARING THE EXACT SAME BANDANNA."

LAZY DAYS ARE THE BEST DAYS.

TOTAL BAMBOO COMA

"UMMM . . . SOMEONE'S IN HERE!"

"YOU PROMISE ALL THE DOGS ARE GONE?"

"WHAT'S THIS I HEAR ABOUT BEING LIFTED UP IN FRONT OF THE ANIMAL KINGDOM?"

"NO WAY! WE'RE OUT OF TOWELS AGAIN?"

"I USED TO FIND
THAT FLEECE RAG
SO ENTERTAINING,
BUT NOW . . ."

"THIS WALKING THING—DO WE HAVE TO?"

"YOU MAY SAY I'M A DREAMER, OR YOU MAY SAY 'HEY! GET OUT OF THE CENTERPIECE.'"

"I LIED. I'M NOT AN ACCOUNTANT. I KNOW NOTHING ABOUT TAXES."

"OH NO, ARE THOSE . . . NAIL CLIPPERS?!"

"MY NAME IS MR. MITTENS, AND I APPROVE THIS MESSAGE."

"DID YOU SAY THERE'S MEAT LOAF AT HOME?"

"GO AHEAD, MAKE A JOKE ABOUT MY BELL NECKLACE. I'VE HEARD THEM ALL."

GAME, SET, FETCH

HE CONSIDERS EATING CARROTS WITH
NO PAWS HIS GREATEST PARTY TRICK.

2-4: Moderate

A moderate Cute Emergency may involve: Discovering your morning shower has no hot water, missing the train by half a second, or being stuck in line behind someone paying in all pennies. Take a deep breath. Puppies to the rescue!

"SHOULD I TELL HER I PEED ON THE COUCH?"

"A LITTLE PRIVACY, PLEASE? I'M WITH SOMEBODY."

35

LITTLE KNOWN TERRIER FACT:
THEY LOVE TO EAVESDROP.

ARE WE THERE YET?

"BY ALL MEANS, LEAD ME TO WATER."

"WHAT'S THAT, HUMAN?
YOU WANT TO GIVE ME A BATH?
FUN FACT: YOU WILL PAY."

"HANG ON TIGHT, SQUEEZY TOY,
I'LL SAVE YOU!"

YOU DECIDE: IS THIS A YAWN OR A ONE-KITTEN METALLICA COVER BAND?

DAPPER DOGS
GET ALL THE
LADIES.

LIFE IN THE FAST LANE.

SORRY, FOLKS, HE'S NEITHER TEENAGE, MUTANT, NOR NINJA.

"SOMEDAY, ALL OF THIS WILL BE YOURS."

THESE TWO—ALWAYS FORGETTING THEIR HOUSE KEYS.

"APPARENTLY I'M A GOOD PILLOW.
THAT'S WHAT SHE TELLS ME."

THIS MUST BE THE LINE FOR THE NEW iPHONE.

"GOOD NIGHT, MANGLED STUFFED ANIMAL."

"GOOD NIGHT, DOG."

EVEN PIGS NEED THEIR BEAUTY REST.

HE'S DREAMING OF A
MAILMAN'S LEG TALLER
THAN THE EYE CAN SEE.

"JUST A FEW MORE MINUTES . . ."

"TOO . . . MUCH . . . CATNIP . . ."

4-6: High

A high-level Cute Emergency may include: When the top of the pizza box gets mushed into the cheese, when the person in front of you at a concert takes photos with an iPad, or when you nail your head on a cabinet and can only speak in expletives. Rest assured, these sweet animals don't know what any of those words mean. They're here for you.

"IT SEEMS MY QUILLS HAVE FAILED ME."

"JUST HANGING OUT WHILE MY OWNER STARS IN A COMMERCIAL FOR ALLERGY MEDICINE."

(SNIFF SNIFF SNIFF.)

"WAS THERE A YORKIE HERE EARLIER, LIKE ON PAGE FIFTY-NINE?"

"CAN WE GET A POOL?"

"I'M UNDER HERE, MOM. OR DID YOU . . . FORGET?"

HE INSISTS THAT
THIS IS THE REAL
DOWNWARD DOG
POSITION.

BE ONE WITH
THE TENNIS
BALL.

ONLY ONE OF THESE DOGS
GOT A FULL NIGHT'S SLEEP.
CAN YOU GUESS WHICH ONE?

HERE'S HOW YOU SUCCESSFULLY CONVINCE YOUR OWNER TO SHARE HER SANDWICH.

"EXCUSE ME, IS THIS MY NEW NEST?"

THIS BUNNY ASKED HIS
BARBER FOR THE RACH

"I'M ALL EARS . . .
METAPHORICALLY."

"DO YOU HAVE TO TAKE PICTURES RIGHT NOW? I JUST WOKE UP."

HE'S GIVING THE
WHOLE VEGAN
THING A TRY.

73

"CAN I DRIVE?"

"IS THIS THING ON? AHEM . . ."

"AAAT LAAAAAST . . ."

7

"HEY, I DON'T TAKE PICTURES OF *YOU* WHEN YOU'RE EATING."

"I'M NOT GONNA MAKE IT! GO ON WITHOUT ME!"

SOME SAY
THIS WAS THE
INSPIRATION
FOR THE SONG
"SHAKE IT OFF."

IS IT REDUNDANT TO WEAR
FUR WHEN YOU HAVE FUR?

"CALL ME FLOPPY ONE MORE TIME—I DARE YOU!"

"I'D TRADE ME POT OF GOLD FOR A DIFFERENT OUTFIT."

81

"IT TASTES LIKE COLD."

"DOES AN APPLE A DAY KEEP
THE VET AWAY, TOO?"

"OH THAT'S GOOD. THAT REALLY TAKES THE EDGE OFF A BUSY WORKWEEK."

R_X

6-8:
Severe

What constitutes a severe Cute Emergency? Examples include: Dropping your phone in the toilet, the crotch of your favorite pants ripping midday, or when you've waited for two hours at the DMV only to realize you forgot one document at home. Do not panic. Kittens, puppies, hedgehogs—*go!*

♫"I ALWAYS FEEL LIKE SOMEBODY'S WATCHIN' MEEE . . ."♫

"OKAY, I PUT ON THE
BEAR COSTUME.
NOW WHEN DO I
GET TO DIP MY PAW
IN HONEY?"

"IS THIS GOING TO GIVE ME HAT HEAD?"

THIS ANGLE IS KNOWN AS
GOLDFISH EYE-VIEW.

"WHAT DID I TELL YOU ABOUT PERSONAL SPACE?"

"THANKS, CAT. I'M JUST GLAD WE'RE BOTH COMFORTABLE."

THEY'D PREFER IF YOU CALLED IT A HUSKYBACK RIDE.

OH GREAT, THEY FORGOT THEIR
FLOATIES AGAIN.

TURNS OUT PIGLETS CLEAN UP
PRETTY WELL!

"HERE, BIG GUY, LET ME HELP YOU FINISH THAT BITE."

"OKAY, YOU CAN COME INTO OUR FORT, BUT NO GERBILS ALLOWED."

"THIS IS MY SLEEPING HAT. GOOD NIGHT."

HE TUCKERED HIMSELF OUT TRYING
TO ROAR.

"I GIVE UP."

"WHAT'S IT LIKE TO PEE OUT THERE?"

"I'M NOT SLEEPING, I'M JUST RESTING
   MY EYES . . .
   AND MY HEAD . . .
   OKAY, I'M SLEEPING."

"I MUST SAY, YOUR FUR LOOKS AMAZING. WHO PICKS IT?"

"IN MY DREAMS, I'M A FLYING SQUIRREL."

"PERFECT. NOW CAN YOU JUST KEEP YOUR HAND THERE FOR THE NEXT SEVEN HOURS?"

IT'S CALLED
CATNAPPING FOR
A REASON.

YOU'RE SAFE FOR NOW, SALMON.

A QUICK AND EASY AT-HOME
FACE-LIFT.

"WAKE ME UP WHEN DINNER'S READY."

LUCKY FOR A SLEEPY HEDGEHOG,
QUILLS ARE BASICALLY
A BUILT-IN "DO NOT
DISTURB" SIGN.

GORILLAS MAY NOT EAT WITH
UTENSILS, BUT THEY KNOW HOW
TO SPOON.

"SORRY I ATE YOUR BOOKMARK."

RX

9+: Extreme

This is where it gets serious. An extreme Cute Emergency may mean you're going through a painful breakup, getting a root canal, or experiencing a sudden power outage during the Puppy Bowl. These adorable animals have been expertly selected for this kind of emergency. (It's a tough job, but somepuppy's gotta do it.)

SIGNATURE _____

WHEN YOU SEE YOUR
OWNER OPENING A
CAN OF TUNA.

"I GOTTA SAY, YOUR LOAFER TASTES ESPECIALLY FLAVORFUL TODAY! WHAT'D YOU STEP IN?"

DENIM IS THE NEW
VELVETEEN.

"NOBODY EVER TELLS ME WHERE WE'RE GOING."

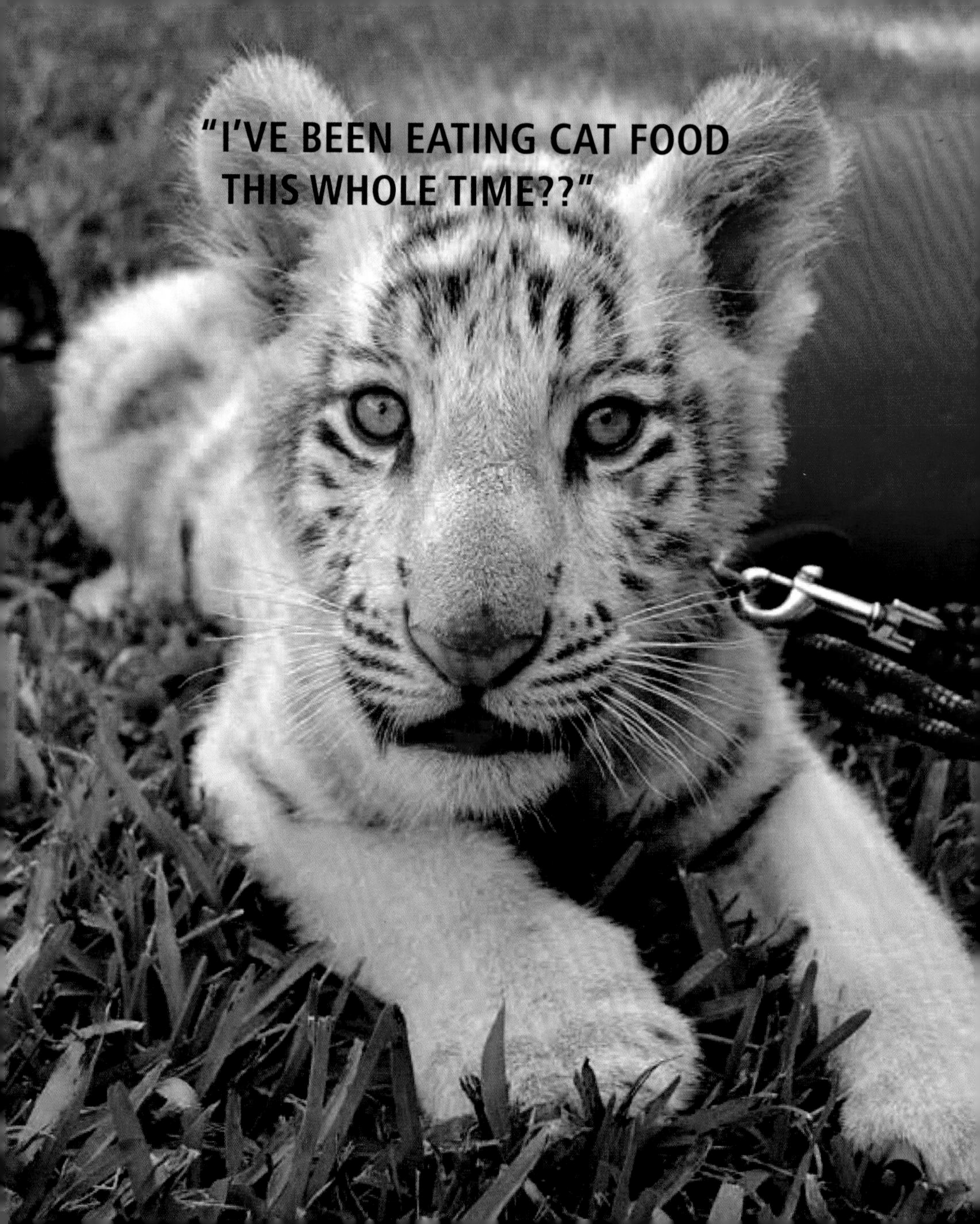
"I'VE BEEN EATING CAT FOOD
THIS WHOLE TIME??"

PLEASE, CALL IT FOLIAGE. "DEAD LEAVES" MAKES HIM SAD.

HIS TEAM LOST THE
PUPPY BOWL.

"IS THERE SOMETHING ON YOUR MIND, HONEY?"

"AM I CAMOUFLAGED? HOW ABOUT NOW?"

DOGGY PADDLING,
HE'S A NATURAL.
SURFING,
NOT SO MUCH.

HE SWEARS HIS ALL-LETTUCE DIET
BEGINS TOMORROW.

MY, WHAT A HAIRY
BABY YOU HAVE.

"I HOPE THIS MAKES YOU SMILE, BECAUSE HE'S LITERALLY MAKING ME SMILE."

131

"I'M SORRY TO SAY I CANNOT RECOMMEND THE SAND SANDWICH."

"LOWER . . . LOWER . . . OH, THAT'S THE SPOT."

LOOKS LIKE SOMEONE JUST DISCOVERED A BANANA PLANTATION.

BE OPEN-MINDED. HAY IS
FOR HORSES *AND* YAKS.

HE'LL BURY A BONE FASTER THAN YOU CAN SAY "RED ROVER."

"LICENSE AND REGISTRATION, PLEASE."

"I OVERHEARD SOME RUSTLING AND THOUGHT PERHAPS THERE WERE SNACKS, THAT'S ALL."

"DID THAT HUMAN CHILD JUST CALL ME 'GRANDMA'?"

ONE TIME HE THOUGHT HE WAS GETTING EATEN BY A MONSTER, BUT IT WAS JUST A MIRROR.

"YOU DRESSED ME LIKE A LITTLE SAILOR. AND YOU KNOW I HATE WATER. GREAT."

THEY'RE NOT
HER KITTENS;
SHE JUST NEEDS
THE BABYSITTING
MONEY.

"THIS IS THE GREATEST
DAY OF MY LIIIFE!"

"ONE DAY, I'LL TEACH YOU HOW TO FLING POOP."

"THE HUMAN IS BEGINNING TO VACUUM. WE MUST SEEK SHELTER FAST."

"ONE OF THESE DAYS, I'M GONNA BUST US OUTTA THIS JOINT."

HE WEARS HIS
HEART ON HIS
NOSE (BECAUSE
HE DOESN'T HAVE
SLEEVES).

THERE'S A WHOLE WORLD OF
GARBAGE CANS FOR THEM TO TOPPLE.

"UGH, MY SISTER IS SUCH A HAM."

"WHAT'S HAPPENING? ARE WE TURNING INTO POLAR BEARS?"

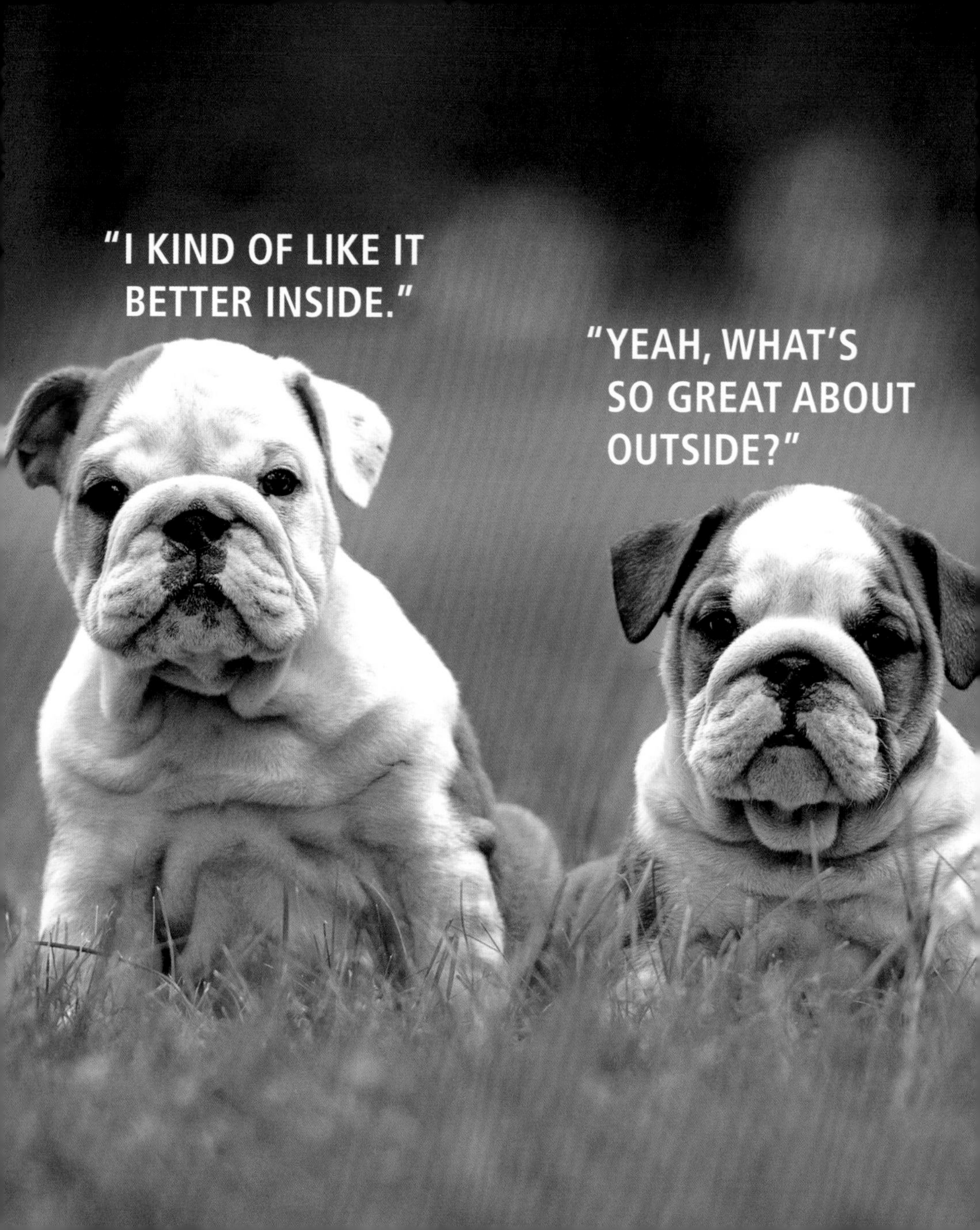
"I KIND OF LIKE IT BETTER INSIDE."
"YEAH, WHAT'S SO GREAT ABOUT OUTSIDE?"

KOALAS SLEEP UP
TO TWENTY HOURS
A DAY. THIS IS ONE
OF THOSE HOURS.

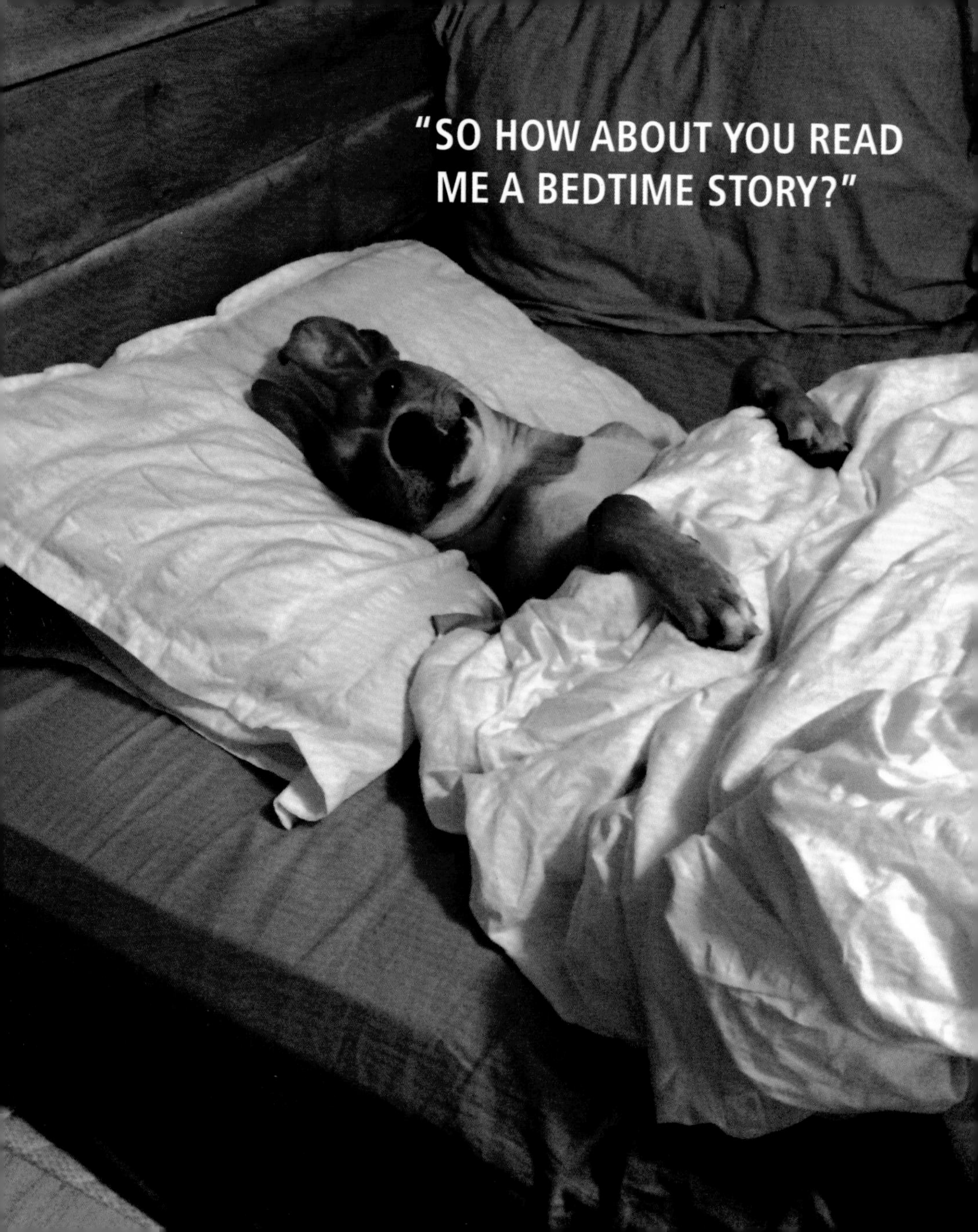
"SO HOW ABOUT YOU READ ME A BEDTIME STORY?"

THIS IS EITHER CUDDLING OR STRANGLING. LET'S GO WITH CUDDLING.

THIS IS WHAT'S KNOWN AS
"MONDAY MORNING FACE."

CAN HE JOIN YOUR MARIACHI BAND NOW?

"IS IT ME OR ARE ALL THE CLOUDS SHAPED EXACTLY LIKE RAWHIDE BONES?"

THEY'RE COPING PRETTY WELL WITH THE PILLOW SHORTAGE.

"WELL, I GUESS I'M LAUNDRY NOW."

AFTERWORD

See, don't things feel better and brighter now?
It's amazing what a few cute animals can do.
Next time you're feeling down or stressed out,
declare it a state of Cute Emergency—because
you may not always have a puppy or a baby
orangutan handy, but you definitely have this
book.

ACKNOWLEDGMENTS

I want to thank everyone who contributed to this book. Without you, it wouldn't have been possible. I'd also like to thank those who helped and supported me in its creation, including Emmy Blotnick, Michelle, Polly, and the Three Rivers Press team. Also, my puppy, Tug, who motivates me every day to get my work done so we can go on walks together.

PHOTO CREDITS

112: Haley Meldrim

113: Gino Sulla

116: Haley Johnson

119: Stephanie Gonzales

121: Shannon Campbell

122: Ashley Marcellus

123: Charlotte Sarkos

124: Adrienne Ciccone

125: Breanna Galley

126–27: Annie Gehlhaus

128: Kate Cahill

129: Hunter Martin

130: Camilla DeCaria

132–33: Nicole Chakirelis

134: Nathan Wolf

136–37: Kendall Fisha

138: Sam Swain

139: LIzzie van der Walde

140: Haley Brust

142: Zack Pittmon

143: Larissa Lucena

147: Kirsty Crowther

148–49: Micaela Alcaino

150: Kayla Vigliotti

152: Angel Meriweather

156: Lauren Alley

157: Taylor Foster

160: Camille Elsea

161: Caroline Corson

Shutterstock: 2, 6, 8, 12, 13, 14, 17, 37 (both), 39, 40, 45, 47, 48–49, 50, 51, 52–53, 58, 59, 62–63, 65, 73, 78, 80, 84–85, 86, 89, 90, 91, 92, 93, 98–99, 102, 103, 104, 106–07, 108, 109, 110, 111, 114, 115, 118, 120, 131, 135, 141, 144, 145, 146, 151, 153, 154, 155, 158, 159, 162

ABOUT THE AUTHOR

TONY HEALLY is the creator of @CuteEmergency, as well as other popular animal-related Twitter accounts, such as @EmrgencyKittens and @OhMyCorgi. Wanting to start a Twitter account to cheer people up, he found that Tweeting about animals was the perfect idea. Since then, @CuteEmergency has made more than 1.5 million people smile.